Developed and produced by Ivor Claydon Graphics
Edited by David Notley

First published in the United Kingdom in 1998

This edition first published in the United Kingdom in 2026 by
Pitkin
43 Great Ormond Street
London
WC1N 3HZ

An imprint of B. T. Batsford Holdings Limited

Copyright © B. T. Batsford Ltd 2026

All rights reserved. No part of this publication may be copied, displayed, extracted, reproduced, utilized, stored in a retrieval system or transmitted in any form or by any means, electronic, mechanical or otherwise including but not limited to photocopying, recording, or scanning without the prior written permission of the publishers.

ISBN 978 1 83733 071 3

A CIP catalogue record for this book is available from the British Library.

1/26

Reproduction by Rival Colour Ltd, UK
Printed and bound by Toppan Leefung International Ltd, China

This book can be ordered direct from the publisher at www.batsfordbooks.com, or try your local bookshop.

Distributed throughout the UK and Europe by Abrams & Chronicle Books, 1st Floor, 22–24 Ely Place, London EC1N 6TE and 57 rue Gaston Tessier, 75166 Paris, France

www.abramsandchronicle.co.uk
info@abramsandchronicle.co.uk

WARTIME RECIPES

45 TASTY AND NUTRITIOUS RECIPES FROM THE
DIG FOR VICTORY YEARS

PITKIN

Contents

SOUPS
PAGE 8

MAIN MEALS
PAGE 14

VEGETABLE COOKERY
PAGE 27

SWEETS AND PUDDINGS
PAGE 34

GIVE THEM BEANS

Look ahead to next winter and plant beans now. Haricots are the best kind. You'll be glad to have a store of them. They are fine food and a clever cook can work wonders with them.

Victorian Scotch Broth

4 carrots
3 turnips
3 onions
2.2 litres/4 pints of water or vegetable stock
75g/3oz pearl barley
1 teaspoonful of chopped parsley
Salt and pepper

Wash, peel and dice the vegetables, put the water or stock into a saucepan and bring to the boil, add the vegetables. Wash the barley and add, let all simmer till the vegetables are soft and barley cooked. Season, sprinkle the parsley in the bottom of a tureen, pour the boiling soup on to it and serve.
Cooking Time: 1½ hours/8 Helpings

Haricot Soup

450g/1lb haricot beans
1 onion
2 small potatoes
1.1 litres/2 pints of vegetable stock or water
150ml/¼ pint milk (if liked)
Seasoning

Wash the beans and soak overnight in cold water. Put into a pan with the stock and the water they were soaked in. Let it come to the boil. Skim. Wash, peel and slice the vegetables and add. Simmer all gently for two hours or till the beans are tender. Rub all through a sieve. Add the milk. Return to the pan and boil. Season and serve.
Cooking Time: 3 hours/6 Helpings

Potato Soup

450g/1lb of peeled potatoes
1 onion
A little fat
900ml/1 1/2 pints of water
Pepper and salt
300ml/1/2 pint milk

Cut up the potatoes, slice the onion and just brown it in a little fat. Add the potatoes and water, pepper and salt to taste, bring to the boil and simmer for two hours. Pass through a sieve, add 300ml/1/2 pint of milk and make very hot.
Cooking Time: 3 hours/6 Helpings

Barley Soup

50g/2oz of pearl barley
450g/1lb carrots and turnips
A sprig of parsley
A small piece of celery
2 good-sized onions
Salt and pepper
Sufficient water to make in all 2.2 litres/4 pints
300ml/1/2 pint of milk

Cover the barley with water and soak overnight. Put it into a casserole with the carrots and turnips sliced, adding the parsley, celery, onions, salt, pepper and water. Bring it to the boil and simmer very gently until the barley is done. Rub it through a wire sieve, add 300ml/1/2 pint of milk, bring it to the boil again and serve.
Cooking Time: 2 hours/8 Helpings

A LITTLE EXTRA WILL MAKE A DIFFERENCE

Try serving some of the following with your favourite soup.

DUMPLINGS
Mix 8oz flour with 1 teaspoonful of baking powder and 1 teaspoonful of dried herbs. Form into a firm dough with cold water. Drop into soup and cook quickly for 10 minutes.

CROUTONS
Take a few slices of wheatmeal bread, dice and bake in a hot oven until crisp.

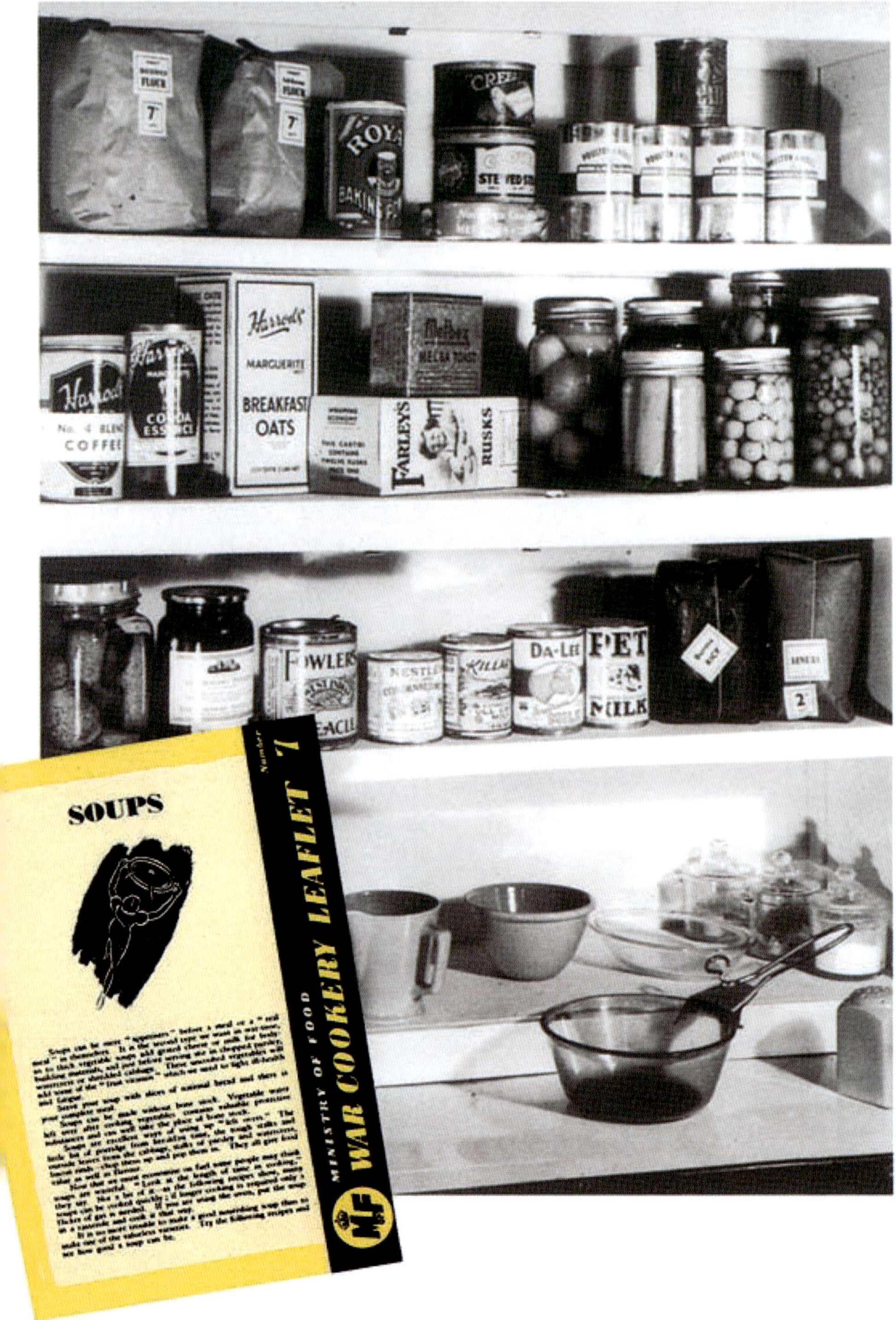
FLOUR
ROYAL
BAKING
STEWED
Harrods
MARGUERITE
BREAKFAST
OATS
No. 4 BLEND
COFFEE
COCOA ESSENCE
FARLEY'S
RUSKS
FOWLERS
TREACLE
NESTLE'S
DA-LEE
PET
MILK
SOUPS
Number 7
MINISTRY OF FOOD
WAR COOKERY LEAFLET
MF

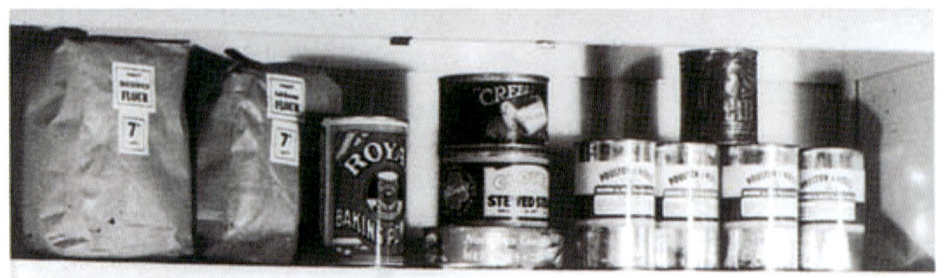

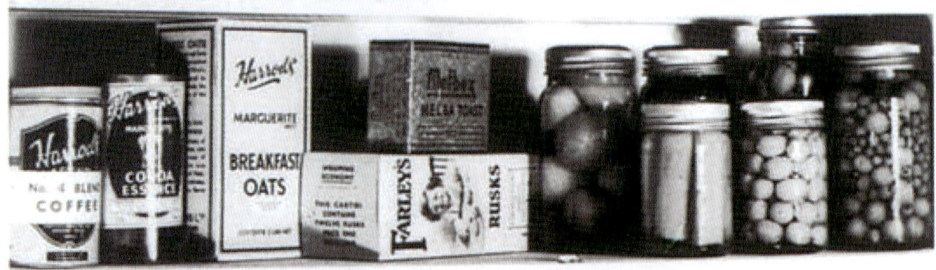

Spinach Soup with Dumplings

450g/1lb spinach
1 turnip
2 onions
1 small head of celery
2 carrots
A little thyme and parsley
600ml/1 pint of stock
12g/½ oz of clarified fat
Pepper and salt
1.1 litres/2 pints of water

Cut up the vegetables and stew all together till tender, pass through a sieve. Add to the vegetable pulp and liquor 1.1litres/2 pints of water, and boil together. Have ready 2 small dumplings for each person, put them in the tureen and pour the boiling soup on to them and serve.
Cooking Time: 2 hours/4 Helpings

Dumplings

225g/½lb flour
25g/1oz of dripping or any fat
Water and salt

Rub the dripping into the flour, add salt. Moisten with a little water, form into balls the size of a marble and drop into boiling water or stock; cook about for 30 minutes.
Cooking Time: 30 minutes/8 Helpings

We are a beleaguered nation, and in our plans for food the overriding objective, indeed the only objective worth considering, is to provide a national diet which will maintain everybody in health.

WARTIME RECIPES

IF AN AIR RAID SIGNAL TAKES YOU FROM THE KITCHEN

First thing to do is to stop the heat, turn off the gas or electric or close the dampers of the kitchen range. If you do this the food cannot get burnt.

Parsnip Soup

4 parsnips
1 onion
1.7 litres/3 pints of good stock
Some well-scaled bacon rinds, if available
25g/1oz of fat
25g/1oz of rice
Salt and pepper
A pinch of ground mace

Chop the onion finely and fry in the fat, then add the parsnips, which should have been washed and grated, then the rice, stock and bacon rinds. Bring to the boil, season and simmer gently for 1½ hours. Test, season again if required, remove the bacon rinds, put through a sieve and serve very hot. Turnip soup may be made in the same way, and if a little milk can be allowed it improves the soup. Too much soft food is not good for the digestion, therefore some cubes of fried bread or toast crusts well browned in the oven should be served with the soup.

Cooking Time: 2 hours/6 Helpings

Gravy Soup

900g/2lb shin of beef
450g/1lb onions or leeks
½ tin tomatoes
450g/1lb carrots or 1 tin (use liquid as stock)
100g/¼lb fat
75g/3oz flour
2.2 litres/4 pints stock or water
Salt and pepper

The Ministry of Food wants your cooking secrets

Shred or chop vegetables and fry in the fat until a golden brown. Add flour and brown. Add meat, cut into small pieces; add liquid slowly. Season and cook slowly for 3 to 4 hours, adding tomatoes 30 minutes before serving, and a little colouring if necessary. Strain through a sieve or colander and re-heat.
Cooking Time: 4 hours/10 Helpings

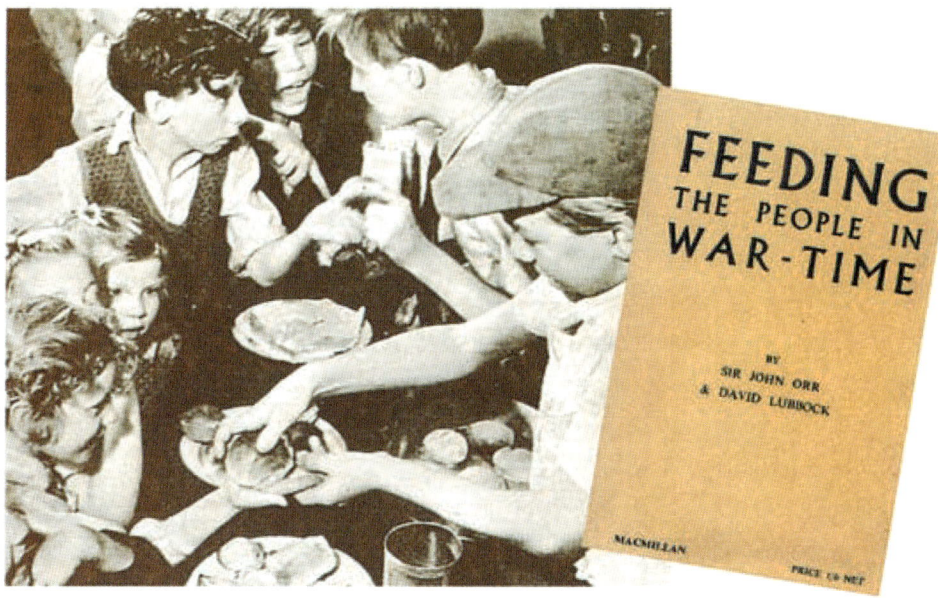

WARTIME RECIPES

There are some recipes here for cooking such things as liver, tripe, kidneys and so on. There are some suggestions for cooking the cheaper cuts of meat.

Beef Hash

**450g/1lb cold salt beef
450g/1lb cold cooked potatoes
Milk
Salt and pepper
1 onion, finely chopped
25g/1oz margarine**

Mince the salt beef and mix it with the cold potatoes, which should be crumbled but not mashed, and finely chopped onion. Season with salt and pepper, add enough milk to moisten, and stir until all are well mixed together. Make the margarine hot in a large frying pan. Spread the mixture all over the pan and put over a low gas, where it can cook slowly. Cook gently for 40-45 minutes. Loosen with a knife and turn on to a hot dish, folding the mixture in two.
Cooking Time: 1 hour/6-8 Helpings

MAIN MEALS

Devilled Fish

225g/8oz cold cooked fish
1 hard-boiled egg, sliced or chopped
37g/1 ½ oz stale breadcrumbs
Pinch of cayenne
Pinch of grated nutmeg
Pinch of curry powder
½ teaspoonful made mustard
2 teaspoonfuls Worcester sauce or tomato ketchup
25g/1oz margarine
25g/1oz flour
300ml/½ pint of milk
Salt and pepper

Trade considerations and many of our food likes and dislikes will have to go by the board. With sufficient milk, vegetables and potatoes, there need be no malnutrition. With sufficient bread, fat (butter or margarine), potatoes and oatmeal, there will be no starvation.

Flake the fish and remove skin and bones. Brush a pie-dish with melted margarine. Melt 25g/1oz of margarine in a saucepan, stir in the flour and cook till it bubbles. Take off the heat and add 300ml/½ pint of milk or milk and water. Bring to the boil, lower the heat and cook for 3 minutes, stirring all the time. Add the fish, egg, nutmeg, curry powder, cayenne, mustard and Worcester sauce or ketchup. Taste, and season with salt and pepper. Pour into prepared dish, coat with breadcrumbs, and bake for 20 minutes in a moderately hot oven.
Cooking Time: 2 hours/ 4-6 Helpings

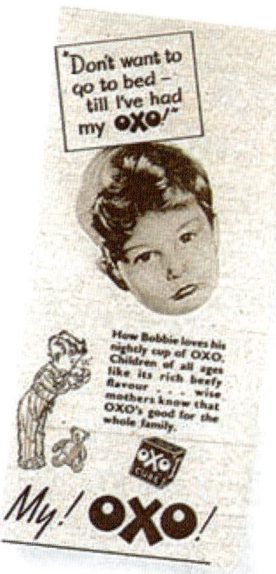

WARTIME RECIPES

Roast Hearts

2 sheep's hearts
1 tablespoonful breadcrumbs
1 teaspoonful shredded suet
Salt and pepper
A little milk
Dripping
1 level tablespoonful self-raising flour
Parsley

Mix the breadcrumbs, seasoning, parsley and salt, and bind with a little milk. Wash the hearts thoroughly, cut away the pipes from the top and cut the dividing walls. Stuff the hearts, fold the flaps over and keep in place with a skewer.
Heat sufficient dripping in a strong saucepan to come 12mm/^{1}/2 inch up the sides. Put in the hearts and brown them all over, reduce the heat and cook gently for 1 hour, turning from time to time. Lift out the hearts, strain off most of the fat and make the gravy by sprinkling a level tablespoonful of self-raising flour into the fat. Stir until brown, season and add vegetable water or hot water. Stir and bring to the boil.
Cooking Time: 2 hours/2 Helpings

The combined effect of propaganda and fall in price is well seen in the case of fruit. In 1900, the price of a banana was 2d. By 1937, it had fallen to 1d. The consumption of bananas between these dates increased from 2^1/2 million to 20 million bunches. In 1920-3, the average price of grapefruit was 6d. By 1935, it had fallen to 3d. The annual consumption increased from 1,200 tons to 59,500 tons. The fall in price was accompanied by the 'eat more fruit' campaign.

FOOD FACTS

It should be remembered that to prepare such cuts of meat as neck of mutton, knuckle of veal, or skirt of beef, the best method is slow long cooking.

Tripe and Onions

450g/1lb tripe
2 large onions
Salt and pepper
600ml/1 pint milk and water
25g/1oz self-raising flour

Bring the onions to the boil, then slice thinly. Wash the tripe thoroughly and cut into pieces. Put the tripe and onions in a saucepan, season and cover with the milk and water. Simmer for 2 hours. Mix the flour to a smooth paste with a little milk, then stir this paste into the tripe and onions. Stir and boil for 5 minutes and serve. Cooking Time: 3 hours/6 Helpings

Corned Beef Rissoles

100g/4oz corned beef
225g/8oz mashed potatoes
225g/8oz cooked mixed vegetables
100g/4oz wheatmeal breadcrumbs
seasoning
pinch mixed herbs
4 tablespoons brown sauce or vegetable water

Crumb the corned beef and mix with the mashed cooked vegetables and breadcrumbs. Season and add the mixed herbs. Bind the mixture with brown sauce or vegetable water, form into round shapes. Bake in a hot oven.
Cooking Time: 20 minutes/2-3 Helpings

Fillets of Pork

225g/8oz pork sausagemeat
225g/8oz potatoes
Pinch of sage
100g/4oz breadcrumbs
150ml/¼ pint vegetable stock
1 tablespoon of flour
Pepper and salt

Flake the pork sausagemeat (with the outside fat removed), then mix in the mashed potatoes and crisp breadcrumbs. Season well with pepper and salt, adding a pinch of sage if liked. Then bind with a thick sauce made from the meat juices taken from the tin, and made up to 1 teacup measure with vegetable stock and flour plus a little of the pork fat from the tin. Divide into nine or ten sections, shape into finger rolls, coat in more crumbs, and fry or bake until heated through and crisp-coated, with a light greasing of pork fat for the frying pan or baking tin.

These are delicious by themselves, or served with Leek Sauce.
Cooking Time: 2 hours/6 Helpings

RECIPE of the WEEK

Leek Sauce
½ pint milk and water
half a leek, chopped
Salt and pepper
1oz flour
Pinch of herbs

Put some of the milk, or milk and water, leek and seasoning into a pan and allow to simmer slowly for 15 to 20 minutes. Blend the flour with the remaining cold milk, stir into the pan with the leek, etc., and cook for 1-2 minutes.

Mince Slices

225g/8oz mince (any cooked meat)
100g/4oz cooked mashed potatoes
100g/4oz stale breadcrumbs
Salt and pepper

Mix well together the mince, mashed potatoes, breadcrumbs and salt and pepper. Turn out onto a floured board and roll into an oblong, ¼ inch thick. Cut into slices and fry in a small quantity of hot fat, or grill for 5-7 minutes. Serve with mashed potatoes and a green vegetable.
Cooking Time: 1 hour/4-6 Helpings

Savoury Meat Roll

350g/12oz sausage meat
100g/4oz stale bread
125g/5oz pinto beans, cooked and mashed
Pepper and salt
1 teaspoon made mustard
1 teaspoon thyme
Gravy browning
Breadcrumbs

Soak the stale bread in water until soft. Squeeze out the water and mash the bread with the sausage meat, the mashed beans, pepper, salt, made mustard and thyme. Add gravy browning until the mixture is a rich brown. Press very firmly into a greased 2lb stone jam jar or tin and steam for 2 hours. Roll in browned breadcrumbs and serve hot with brown gravy, or cold with a raw cabbage heart salad and boiled potatoes.
Cooking Time: 3 hours/6 Helpings

American Mince

150g/6oz corned beef, minced or finely chopped
225g/8oz cooked pearl barley
1/2 pint tomato pulp
salt and pepper
25g/1oz cheese, grated
25g/1oz breadcrumbs
12g/1/2 oz dripping or margarine
2 tomatoes (if available)

Place the beef, barley, tomato pulp, seasoning, cheese and breadcrumbs in layers in a greased pie dish. Finish with a layer of cheese and dot with the dripping or margarine. Bake in a moderate oven for 25 minutes. Slice the whole tomatoes and spread over the top. Return to the oven for a further 15 minutes.
Cooking Time: 1 hour/4-6 Helpings

Liver and Bacon with Rice

450g/1lb liver
225g/8oz rice
225g/8oz bacon
150ml/¼ pint of good stock
150ml/1 tablespoonful of flour

Fry the bacon and then remove and keep hot. Then fry the sliced liver in the bacon fat until brown. Remove and keep hot. Add and stir the flour to the pan juices, before adding the stock, salt and pepper. Stir until the sauce begins to boil. Have ready a good dish of boiled rice, arrange the liver and bacon on it and pour the sauce over the top.
Cooking Time: 1 hour/6 Helpings

Smothered Sausages

225g/8oz sausages
1lb mashed potatoes
Salt and pepper
150ml/¼ pint of hot milk
1 tablespoonful chopped parsley
1oz margarine

Put the sausages in a saucepan of cold water and bring to the boil. Remove the skins and put each sausage in flour. Brush a fireproof dish with melted margarine, lay the sausages in and sprinkle with salt and pepper. Boil the potatoes and mash adding a knob of margarine, the hot milk and beat well. Season well and spread over the sausages. Brush with a little milk and decorate with a fork. Bake for 30 minutes in a hot oven.
Cooking Time: 1 hour/4 Helpings

Beef à la Mode

675g/1 1/2lb stewing steak
2 large onions
3 carrots
2 bay leaves
50g/2oz margarine
2 tablespoonfuls of vinegar
Salt and pepper
2 cloves

Lay the pieces of beef in a deep dish. Cut the onions and carrots in slices and lay them with the cloves and bay leaves on top of the meat. Pour the vinegar over the meat and leave it to soak overnight. Heat the margarine in a casserole, put in the meat and cook first on one side, then on the other. Put in the onions, carrots, bay leaves, salt and pepper to taste and add enough cold water to just cover the meat. Cook on a gentle heat for 5 hours. This long cooking is necessary either on a ring or oven for the success of the dish.
Cooking Time: 6 hours/6-8 Helpings

Savoury Tripe Casserole

225g/8oz tripe
1 sheep's kidney
100g/4oz calf's liver
25g/1oz margarine
1 carrot, cut into slices
1 onion, sliced
1 bay leaf
1 tablespoonful flour
Salt and pepper
$^1/_2$ teaspoonful mixed herbs

Cut the tripe into strips and the liver into slices. Wash the kidney, remove the fat and cut into small pieces. Mix the flour, season generously with salt and pepper together with the herbs. Toss the tripe, liver and kidneys in the seasoned flour. Melt the margarine in a casserole dish and make it hot. Put in the meat, the carrot and onion and fry together for a few minutes. Pour in enough boiling water just to cover the ingredients, add the bay leaf and simmer gently over a low heat, or in a moderate oven for 2 hours. Serve hot in the casserole with dumplings if you wish.
Cooking Time: 3 hours/6 Helpings

MAIN MEALS

WARTIME RECIPES

Savoury Onions

4 medium onions
50g/2oz cheese, grated
Salt and pepper
1 egg or 1 reconstituted egg
½ teacupful soft breadcrumbs
12g/½oz melted margarine
1 teaspoonful chopped sage

Peel the onions, put into boiling salted water and cook steadily for 30 minutes. Lift the onions out of the liquid, save ½ teacup of this. Remove the centres of the onions, chop this finely and blend with the breadcrumbs, sage, cheese and egg. Season the mixture and fill the onion cases then put these into a casserole with ½ teacup of onion stock. Brush the onions with the melted margarine. Cover the casserole and bake for 45 minutes in the centre of a moderately hot oven.
Cooking Time: 2 hours/4 Helpings

Turnip Top Salad

100g/4oz turnip tops
100g/4oz white cabbage heart
50g/2oz raw beetroot
50g/2oz raw carrots
Salad dressing
Watercress for garnishing

Grate or shred all the vegetables separately and arrange attractively on a large dish. Sprinkle with salad dressing and decorate with watercress. Make the salad dressing by adding vinegar, a little mustard, pepper and salt to a white sauce.
Cooking Time: 20 minutes/6 Helpings

SALAD SUGGESTIONS

Well-shredded spinach, heart of cabbage, leaves of spring greens, make a delicious salad base. And you've no idea until you try them how tasty young dandelion leaves can be. Choose young leaves, wash, chop finely and mix with any raw shredded root vegetables. A little sugar is a help in this kind of salad.

WARTIME RECIPES

FOOD FACTS

It is worthwhile considering alternatives to meat dishes these days. Recipes containing different forms of body-building material, such as cheese, beans and lentils can be served either as an extra dish, or as the main dish of the meal.

Pathfinder Pudding

SUET PASTRY
150g/6oz national flour
1/2 teaspoonful salt
3/4 teaspoonful baking powder
25g/1 oz suet, chopped or grated
40g/1 1/2 oz uncooked potato, shredded
Water
FILLING
900g/2lb cooked parsnips, diced
100g/4oz cheese, grated
1 uncooked leek, sliced
1/2 teaspoon mustard powder
Pepper
1 teaspoon salt

Mix the flour, salt and baking powder, add the suet, potato and water to bind. Roll out three-quarters of the pastry to line a 1.1 litre/2 pint greased basin. Mix the parsnips, cheese, leek, mustard, pepper and salt together. Put into the lined basin. Roll out the remaining quarter of pastry to form a lid. Put this into the pudding, cover with an up-turned saucer and steam for 2 hours.
Cooking Time: 3 hours/6-8 Helpings

Vegetable Casserole

450g/1lb each of potatoes, onions and carrots
450g/1lb cooked haricot beans
450g/1lb tomatoes
1 large cauliflower
225g/½lb cooked macaroni or spaghetti
2.2 litres/4 pints of water
100g/4oz margarine

Wash and peel the potatoes and carrots and cut them into smallish pieces. Peel and slice the onions. Wash the cauliflower, pull off all the florets and slice the stalk and the green leaves. Put into a casserole with the margarine, add salt and water. Bring to the boil and simmer gently for 40 minutes. After 20 minutes, add the tomatoes and the cooked haricots. Cook the macaroni separately in boiling salted water and put into the stew, season and serve.
Cooking Time 2 hours/12 Helpings

Vegetable Casserole

DOs AND DON'Ts WITH VEGETABLES

DO serve swedes when greens are short, or for a change. Of all the root vegetables, swedes are rich in Vitamin C.

DO provide at least one pound of potatoes per head every day and less bread.

DO cook potatoes in their skins, this prevents their goodness dissolving into the water.

DO serve something green and raw every day.

DON'T soak vegetables long, their vitamins and minerals seep out into the water.

DON'T throw vegetable water away, use it for soups and sauces.

VEGETABLE MIXTURES

Here are some good vegetable mixtures which will be popular now that we may have to eat more vegetables than we did:

1 Baked or steamed potatoes, baked or boiled onions and brussels sprouts.

2 Cauliflower and carrots, cooked separately, but served together.

3 Potatoes baked in their jackets, and carrots or parsnips par-boiled and baked in the oven with a little margarine until they are brown.

4 Carrots, swedes and turnips, all mashed together with hot milk.

Tomato Macaroni au Gratin

225g/8oz macaroni
½ tin tomatoes
100g/4 oz cheese
1 small onion, chopped
50g/2oz margarine
3 springs of parsley
Salt and pepper
1 tablespoonful stale breadcrumbs

Brush a deep pie dish with melted margarine. Cook the macaroni in boiling water for 20 minutes, then test a piece between the teeth. If it is soft, drain off the water (which should be kept to make sauce or soup). While the macaroni is cooking, melt the margarine in a saucepan, cook the chopped onion in it until soft, draw the pan off the heat, add the tomatoes, parsley, salt and pepper and leave the mixture to simmer for 30 minutes. Then put the macaroni into the saucepan with the sauce, season with salt and pepper, add the grated cheese and stir well. Turn into the prepared dish and scatter the breadcrumbs over the top. Put into a quick oven for 15 minutes at 210°C (425°F or Mark 7) and serve hot.

Cooking Time: 2 hours/6-8 Helpings

The Ministry of Food wants your cooking secrets

VEGETABLE COOKERY

Mock Duck

450g/1lb red lentils
2 large onions
½ teaspoonful of sage
½ teaspoonful sweet herbs
100g/4oz rice or mashed potatoes
25g/1oz fat
Brown sauce

Wash the lentils, mince and fry the onions lightly, add the lentils, and 2.2 litres/4 pints of stock, bring to the boil and simmer until the lentils are soft. Add the potatoes or rice, sage and herbs, and season well. Shape as much like a duck as possible and place on a greased baking sheet and bake in a hot oven till brown. Baste often. Serve on a hot dish with brown sauce poured round. The lentils will absorb the stock; if they get too dry before they are soft, add more stock. If rice is used instead of potatoes, cook it with lentils. Cooking Time 2 hours/4-6 Helpings

VEGETABLE COOKERY

Potatoes au Gratin

900g/2lb cold cooked potatoes
300ml/½ pint milk
100g/4oz grated cheese
50g/2oz margarine
2 tablespoonfuls stale breadcrumbs
Salt and pepper

Mash the potatoes thoroughly in a saucepan with 300ml/½ pint of boiling milk and 38g/1½ozs margarine. Take the pan from the heat, season with salt and pepper and add the grated cheese. Brush a pie-dish with melted margarine, put the potato mixture into it, smooth it neatly and brush with the remaining margarine, melted. Scatter the stale breadcrumbs over the top and put into a hot oven for 15 minutes.
Cooking Time: 40 minutes/6-8 Helpings

FOOD FACTS

Those who have "dug for victory" will surely be interested in new ways of cooking and serving young carrots, their early peas and new potatoes, not to speak of the wealth of green stuff that will be coming along in late spring and summer.

Caramel and Semolina Mould

50g/2oz sugar
4 tablespoonfuls water
600ml/1 pint milk or milk and water
1 tablespoonful apricot jam or marmalade
75g/3oz semolina

Put the sugar and 2 tablespoons of water into a saucepan, stir until the sugar has dissolved, then boil until a golden caramel. Add the remaining water and heat until blended, cool slightly then pour into a basin or mould. Meanwhile bring the milk or milk and water to the boil in a separate pan, add the jam or marmalade, whisk in the semolina and cook steadily for 10-15 minutes, stirring most of the time. Allow to cool and stiffen slightly, stir briskly then spoon over the caramel and allow to set. Turn out to serve.
Cooking Time: 1 hour/6 Helpings

Eggless Sponge Pudding

150g/6oz self-raising flour or plain flour
1½ teaspoonfuls baking powder
50g/2oz margarine or cooking fat
50g/2oz sugar
1 tablespoonful golden syrup
¼ teaspoonful bicarbonate of soda
1 dessertspoonful vinegar
Milk to mix

Sift the flour or flour and baking powder, rub in the margarine or cooking fat, add the sugar and golden syrup. Blend the bicarbonate of soda with the vinegar, add to the other ingredients, with enough milk to make a sticky consistency. Put the mixture into a greased basin, allowing room to rise. Cover with a plate or margarine paper. Steam for 1¼-1½ hours or until firm. Serve hot with fruit or jam.

VARIATIONS
A little golden syrup or jam could be put into the basin before adding the sponge mixture.
Cooking Time: 2 hours/4-6 Helpings

Bread Pudding

EVERY CRUMB COUNTS
Never throw away stale bread. Use it as breadcrumbs in savoury and sweet puddings, in a breakfast cereal, or crushed for coatings. Soak, squeeze and beat up with a fork for sweet and savoury puddings, etc.

A Bread Pudding is an excellent way to use up bread. The recipe below can be varied in many ways, for example if you are short of dried fruit use a diced cooking apple or a little more marmalade. Slices of Bread Pudding are ideal to tuck into a packed meal box for a factory worker.

225g/8oz stale bread
50g/2oz grated suet
25g/1oz sugar
1 tablespoonful marmalade
50g/2oz dried fruit
1 reconsitituted dried egg
Milk to mix
Ground cinnamon

Put the bread into a basin, add cold water and leave for 15 minutes then squeeze dry with your fingers. Return the bread to the basin, add all the other ingredients, with enough milk to make a sticky consistency. If the spice is added last you can make quite certain you have the right amount. Put into a greased Yorkshire pudding tin and bake in the centre of a slow oven for $1\frac{1}{2}$ hours or steam in a greased basin for 2 hours. Remove from the steamer or oven and allow to cool for 10 minutes. Serve on its own or with custard or condensed milk.
Cooking Time: 3 hours/6 Helpings

Steamed Date Pudding

75g/3oz self-raising flour
50g/2oz stale breadcrumbs
50g/2oz margarine
225g/8oz dates, stoned and chopped
1 tablespoonful golden syrup
1/2 teaspoonful cinnamon and nutmeg
Pinch of salt
150ml/1/4 pint of milk

Brush a pudding basin with melted margarine. Add to the rest of the melted margarine the golden syrup and the milk, heated together. Mix together the flour, breadcrumbs, spices, salt and chopped dates. Pour the milk etc., on to the mixture and stir well until it is moist all through. Put into the prepared basin, cover with doubled paper brushed with melted margarine and steam for 2 1/2 hours. Serve with lemon sauce.
Cooking Time: 3 hours/4-6 Helpings

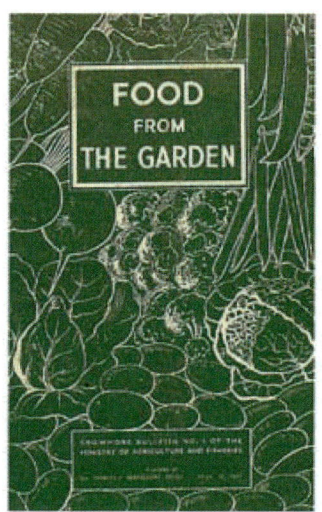

Victory will depend as much on the morale and powers of endurance of the civilian population as on the efficiency of the fighting forces.

Prune Pudding

450g/1lb prunes, soaked in 300ml/½ pint cold water
2 tablespoonfuls golden syrup
Piece of stick cinnamon
450ml/¾ pint boiling water
2 tablespoonfuls lemon juice
100g/4oz cornflour

Soak the prunes overnight. Simmer them in the water they were soaked in with 2 tablespoonfuls of golden syrup. Remove the stones and simmer in the syrup, with the cinnamon and boiling water, for 10 minutes. Blend the cornflour with a little cold water and add to the prune mixture. Boil for 5 minutes stirring all the time. Add the lemon juice, remove the cinnamon and pour into a wetted mould. Leave to set in a mould and serve with thick cream or custard sauce.
Cooking Time: 30 minutes/4-6 Helpings

Prune Pudding

SWEETS AND PUDDINGS

Date and Raisin Pudding

150g/6oz self-raising flour
50g/2oz margarine
50g/2oz dates, stoned and cut into pieces
50g/2oz raisins, stoned
Pinch of bicarbonate of soda
1 teaspoonful golden syrup
Milk to mix
Pinch of salt

Brush a pudding basin and a doubled paper with melted margarine. Sift the flour, carbonate of soda and salt and rub in the margarine. Add the dates and raisins. Mix to a fairly soft consistency with the milk and golden syrup. Put into the prepared basin, cover with prepared paper and steam for 1½ hours. Serve with custard sauce.
Cooking Time: 2 hours/4-6 Helpings

Spotted Dick

225g/8oz self-raising flour
75g/3oz shredded suet
½ teaspoonful salt
50g/2oz sugar
75g/3oz currants
50g/2oz sultanas
Water or milk to mix

Sift the flour and salt into a basin, add the suet, sugar and fruit and mix to a moderately soft dough, with the milk. Put into a greased basin, cover the top with a greased paper and steam for 2½ hours. When cooked turn out and serve with custard.
Cooking Time: 3 hours/6-8 Helpings

Experiment with all your meals as much as you can because it adds variety and does you good.

Apple Cocada

6 cooking apples
100g/4oz desiccated coconut
300ml/½ pint milk
2-4 tablespoonfuls soft brown sugar
25g/1oz margarine

Soak the coconut in milk for an hour. Brush a pie-dish with melted margarine, put a layer of coconut. Peel, core and quarter the apples, put a layer of these into the dish. Sprinkle with sugar and dot with margarine. Repeat these layers once, adding enough sugar to sweeten the apples. Bake for an hour in a moderate oven.
Cooking Time: 2 hours/4-6 Helpings

Honey Walnut Pudding

100g/4oz self-raising flour
50g/2oz stale breadcrumbs
1 egg, beaten
4 tablespoonsful honey
50g/2oz shelled walnuts
50g/2oz margarine
2 teaspoonfuls vanilla essence
1 teacupful milk

Brush a pie dish with melted margarine. With the rest of the melted margarine mix the milk, honey and the beaten egg and warm gently. Mix the flour, breadcrumbs and walnuts, roughly chopped, in a basin. Add the vanilla to the milk mixture and pour it on to the flour, etc. Mix, pour into the pie dish and bake for 1 hour in a warm oven 180°C (350°F or Mark 4). Serve with honey.
Cooking Time: 2 hours/4-6 Helpings

Brown Betty

225g/8oz stale breadcrumbs
900g/2lb apples
2 tablespoonfuls golden syrup
1/4 teaspoonful grated nutmeg
1 teaspoonful cinnamon
50g/2oz margarine
1 teacupful of water
1 lemon

Brush a pie dish with melted margarine. Put a layer of stale breadcrumbs at the bottom. Cover with a layer of grated apples. It is not necessary to peel the apples; they are better grated whole. Put half the golden syrup over the apples. Dot with margarine and sprinkle with the spices, mixed together, and the grated rind of half the lemon. Repeat the layers, and put a final layer of breadcrumbs on top, dotted with margarine. Mix the juice of the lemon with a teacupful of water and pour over the pudding. Bake for 45 minutes in a moderate oven.
Cooking Time: 1 hour/6-8 Helpings

FOOD FACTS

There is thus no need for the public to worry about the food position so far as supplies are concerned. The difficulty in war is the same as it was in peacetime, not one of supply but one of more equal distribution of the food which is available.

WARTIME RECIPES

Coconut Orange Pudding

225g/8oz self-raising flour
75g/3oz margarine
75g/3 tablespoonfuls golden syrup
50g/2oz desiccated coconut
300ml/½ pint milk
1 orange

Rub the margarine into the flour, add the coconut and the grated rind of the orange. Mix the golden syrup with the milk and pour it on the mixture. Prepare a pudding basin or pie dish by brushing it with melted margarine. Put in the pudding mixture, steam for 2 hours, covered with a doubled paper brushed with margarine, or bake for 50 minutes in a moderately hot oven. Serve with the juice of an orange mixed with golden syrup.

Cooking Time: 2 hours/6-8 Helpings

Coconut Orange Pudding

Florida Pudding

450g/1lb stale cake or, better still, gingerbread
1 tin of peaches
25g/1oz desiccated coconut
25g/1oz margarine

Cut the stale cake in square pieces. Put a layer of cake into a pie dish and pour some of the syrup from the peaches over it. Slice the peaches and lay them on top of the cake adding the rest of the syrup. Leave to soak for half an hour, then dot with margarine and sprinkle with coconut. Bake for 1 hour in a moderate oven.
Cooking Time: 2 hours/6 Helpings

Orange Mould

50g/2oz cornflour
600ml/1 pint milk
25g/1oz sugar
Rind and juice of $\frac{1}{2}$ orange
$\frac{1}{2}$ orange for decoration
12g/$\frac{1}{2}$oz margarine

Blend the cornflour with a little cold milk, put the rest of the milk on to boil. When the milk comes to the boil, pour it on to the blended cornflour, stirring well. Add the grated rind of the orange, cut the orange in half and add the juice from one half. Add this also to the cornflour. Return the mixture to the saucepan, add the margarine and boil; boil for five minutes, stirring all the time. Add the sugar and pour into the jelly mould. When cold and set, turn onto a glass dish and decorate with pieces of orange.
Cooking Time: 30 minutes/2 Helpings

Baked Sultana Cake Pudding

225g/8oz pieces of cake
50ml/2oz sultanas
300ml/½ pint milk
1 egg
Sugar to taste

Place a layer of cake in the bottom of a pie dish, brushed with melted margarine, sprinkle with a few sultanas and a little sugar, and repeat these layers until the ingredients are used up. Mix the beaten egg with the milk and pour over the dry ingredients. Bake in a fairly hot oven for 50 minutes. Serve with custard.
Cooking Time: 1 hour/4 Helpings

Lemon Tart

150g/6oz short crust or biscuit crust
3 tablespoonfuls lemon curd (see below)

Make the pastry and roll to a round. Brush a pie plate with melted margarine, fit the round of pastry into it. Spread the lemon curd over it, trim the edges. Roll out the trimmings, cut thin strips from them and decorate the top of the tart. Bake 25-30 minutes in a moderately hot oven.
Cooking Time: 1 hour/4-6 Helpings

FOOD FACTS

EVERY CRUMB COUNTS
Never throw away stale bread. Use it as breadcrumbs in a breakfast cereal, or crush them for coatings. Soak, squeeze and beat up with a fork for sweet and savoury puddings, etc.

Wartime Lemon Curd

25g/1oz margarine
1 level tablespoonful cornflour
2 lemons
150ml/¼ pint water
125g/5oz granulated sugar
1 egg

Peel the rind off the lemons very thinly (a potato peeler is the best thing to use for this purpose). Put the rind into the 150ml/¼ pint of water and bring to the boil. Beat the egg and blend the cornflour with it, taking care to make the mixture smooth; mixing egg and cornflour makes it possible to boil the mixture without curdling the egg. Add the lemon juice and strain the boiling water over the mixture, stirring well. Return to the pan, add the sugar and stir over the heat for 3 minutes. Add the margarine, stir it well in and pour into a basin to cool.
Cooking Time: 30 minutes/10 Helpings

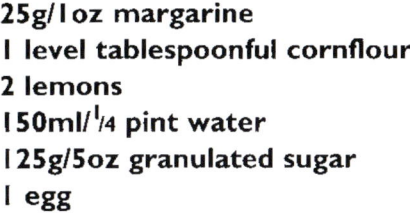